Kids at Work

by
Jeannine B. Browning

8552 Sylvan Drive
Melbourne, Florida 32904-2426

First Printing 4,000 copies April, 1993
Second Printing 7,000 copies June, 1995
ISBN 0-9627729-2-5

AUTHOR AND PUBLISHER — Jeannine Brown Browning
(6 years old)

Cover Artist — Liz Thibodeaux
Artists — Tricia Mast and Liz Thibodeaux

My thanks to my family and friends for their very delicious, entertaining, and touching contributions to Kids at Work.

They are the greatest — Colleen Barton, Richard and Dee Burner, Leah Casper, Julie Casper Clifton, Jane Davies, Sue Fetner, Peggy Gagnon, Carolyn Hazel, Tricia Mast, Charlene Mathews, Jane McElyea, Dee Dee Pannell, Peggy Pifer, Bonnie Sego, Lindy Hazel Taylor and Gee Gee Wood.

Table of Contents

Dedication

This cookbook is dedicated with love and devotion to my six grandchildren. They are everything that they should be, and more. I love each one of them with a love that is complete in every way. They make me happy and sad, they make me laugh and cry, they are everything to me!

ELIZABETH GUTH — May 11, 1981

NICHOLAS GUTH — September 2, 1983

THOMAS GUTH — August 23, 1985

JUSTIN MAST — May 31, 1987

REBECCA MAST — October 29, 1990

SHELBY BROWNING — April 15, 1995

You can't smile without cheering yourself up!

Butterflies

Children are like butterflies
Flitting here and there,
They represent God's beauty
That fills the very air.

They are so very precious
These special gifts from God,
They grow up oh so quickly,
Just close your eyes and nod.

Take time to enjoy your children
These precious, fragile souls,
Just give them love and compassion,
And encouragement to attain life's goals.

Children are like butterflies
So beautiful to see,
These special gifts from God
Mean everything to me.

J. Browning

Tea Time!

My precious childhood memories revolve around little dollies, tricycles, building blocks and cookies! When you say cookies, I say "Tea Time!" You see I was a fortunate little girl who had a Fairy godmother live down the street. I'd put on a clean dress and even wash behind my ears before trotting off to her house. I knew what was waiting for me...cookies, tea and a lot of love. She'd greet me at the door with the tightest, warmest hug I'll ever know. Once in the kitchen I'd climb upon my yellow stool like a little princess on her throne. And thence commenced our tea parties.

We'd chat, woman to little girl who thinks she's a woman, for hours. Most of all, we'd munch and sip, the warmth of the tea warming our hearts. Of course, my time to leave always came much too soon. I'd politely thank her for the treats and never made it to the door without a sweet kiss planted firmly on my cheek.

Those tea parties seem like only yesterday. I can almost still see the rosy pink lip marks on my face. The smell of tea, cookies and her perfume will always remain just a thought away. Even years later she gave me a bigger tea party, my bridal luncheon. I'm sure that won't be the last of them. One day, when I have a little girl of my own, I just may have to take her to meet my special fairy godmother...so she can make some special memories of her own.

I know my memories will always stay warm and alive in the oven of my heart!

I love you, fairy godmother!

Julie Casper Clifton

(This beautiful tribute to our many tea parties and shared love will always live in the oven of my heart, too! Thanks, Julie! — Jeannine)

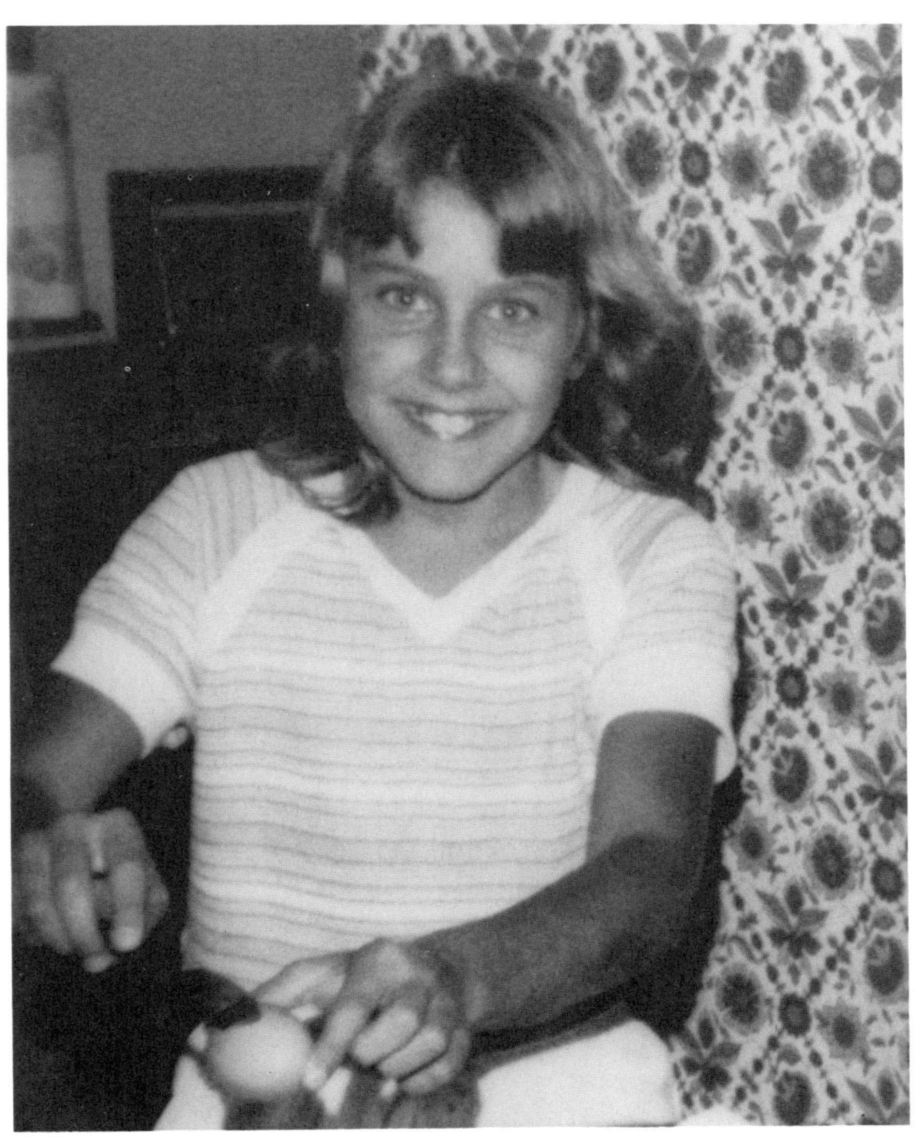

Julie Casper

How To Measure

Measuring is very easy. All you do is fill your measuring spoon with whatever ingredient called for, take the straight side of a table knife and go over the top of the spoon spilling any excess off your spoon. That leaves you with your tablespoon or teaspoon to use in your recipe.

A measuring cup for dry ingredients (flour, sugar, etc.) should be measured in a measuring cup without a lip. It is flat on top and you measure just like you do in a spoon.

A measuring cup for liquids has a spout or lip on it. You measure all liquids (milk, juices, syrup, etc.) in this type of cup. Just add liquid to the correct measuring line. Pour into your recipe as needed.

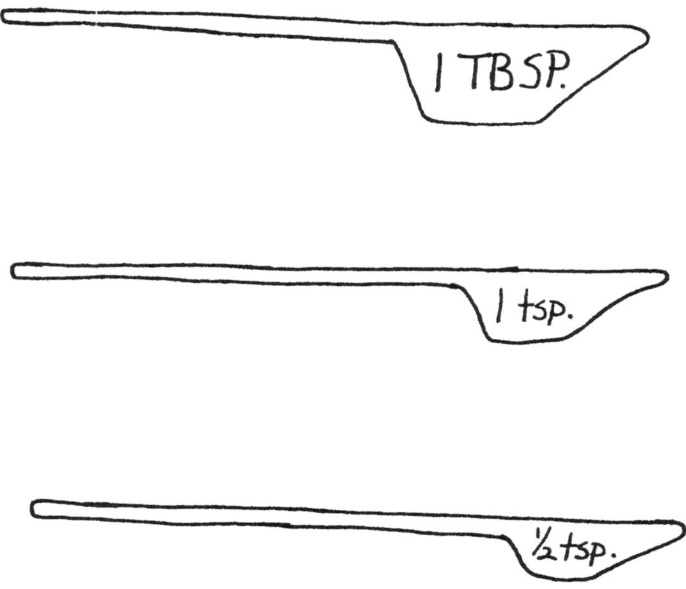

Dry

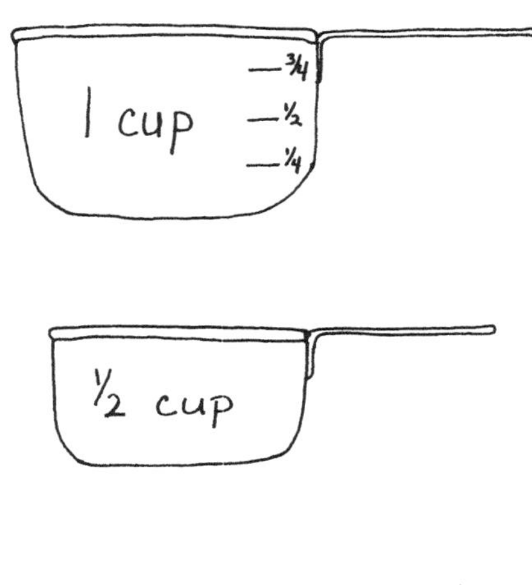

Liquid

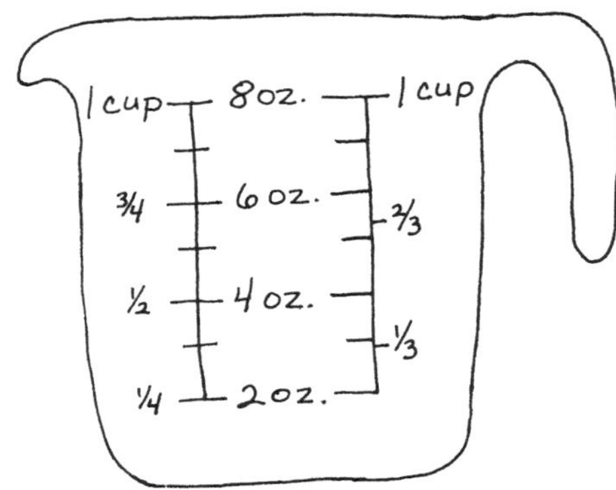

How To Read a Recipe

I know that reading a recipe sounds simple to anyone who can read a book. However, the really important thing about reading a recipe is that you must begin at the beginning and read it all the way through before you begin cooking. The main reason being that you must be sure you know how to do everything the recipe tells you to do, and you must have all the ingredients in your kitchen. Many people begin making a recipe, then read it through and find out they don't have a certain ingredient, then have to stop making it, or go to the grocery store. If you read your recipe through first, check to see that you have all the ingredients in your kitchen, then you are ready to cook.

When you are baking always try to have your eggs, milk and margarine (butter) at room temperature...this means that you take the eggs, milk and margarine required for your recipe out of the refrigerator about one hour before you begin cooking.

If you don't completely understand what something means in a recipe, ask your mother or dad before you begin mixing.

Cooking can be lots of fun. Learn how to cook the right way while you are young and you should be an expert by the time you are an adult.

How to Teach Your Child to Cook

Begin teaching your child how to cook long before they are capable of cooking by themselves. Let them sit on a counter where you are mixing ingredients and help as able. (Make sure they are not seated near a mixer, and that they don't fall off the counter!)

By the time a child is three or four years old they can begin cutting out biscuits, hand cookies, rolled cookies, etc. They may not do a perfect job and may be a little messy, but you can be sure the end results will be the same. Any cookie or biscuit they have cut out and planned for daddy or grandmother, will be absolutely delicious. Perfection is not what you are striving for at this age.

A responsible 8-10 year old should be able to cook some things alone. My best advice to you as a parent is to teach them how to "work" the kitchen.

Begin by teaching your child how to use the oven, oven gloves, mixer and blender. Teach them how to measure dry ingredients and liquid ingredients and how to use measuring spoons. Teach them to always read a recipe through and be certain you have all ingredients before you begin. It is very frustrating to begin cooking a recipe and then find out you don't have a major ingredient. Another very important item to teach your young cook is how to clean up as they go along. Never allow them the pleasure of cooking, and then leaving the dirty dishes for you.

When you feel confident both of you are comfortable with all these things, then go to your room or go outside and stay there until he or she is finished. This may be difficult the first few times, but stick to it. A little praise goes a long way!

I have four children and they are all excellent cooks. They would probably not be such good cooks if I had not followed the above directions. I would probably have "helped" them until they hated cooking. (My theory is that is why so many adults today don't like to cook.) Most recipes will not be ruined if they make a small error on their own. Who knows, perhaps they will have created a new and wonderful recipe!

How to Cook a Complete Meal for your Family

1. Choose a menu where you have an entree (Beef, chicken, fish, etc.), vegetable and salad.

2. Check all menus to be sure you have everything the recipe calls for.

3. If frozen, make sure all ingredients are defrosted.

4. Give yourself plenty of time to cook everything.

5. Set the table while everything is cooking.

6. Decide what you are going to drink and have that ready.

7. Tell your family when you think dinner will be ready (Give yourself plenty of time.)

8. When everyone is finished eating, clean the kitchen and put away any leftover food.

9. Feel proud of yourself! You have done something special!

10. Next time you fix dinner, add a dessert to your menu.

What's That?

Alyson Burner is a special friend of mine and has been since she was a child. Her dad, Richard, gave me this story about Alyson.

One day when Dee (Alyson's mother) was sick in bed, Alyson was home with her and decided to fix her lunch. Alyson busied herself in the kitchen deciding on what to fix. She finally decided on soup. She opened a can of clam chowder and poured the contents into a pan. She added one can of milk, per the instructions on the label, and heated it to simmering. She served it in a bowl on a breakfast tray along with some crackers. It looked good. However, it tasted awful! Her mother could not eat it.

Later Richard and Dee reviewed the making of the chowder with Alyson: empty the can into pan; add one can of milk; heat. What about the milk? Alyson said she had trouble finding a can of milk; she looked everywhere for one. She finally found one can of milk on the back of one of the shelves in the pantry; a can of sweetened condensed milk.

I tell you this story for two reasons. First, it is funny! Second, because it is a good lesson for each person reading this book and planning on cooking.

Usually you will deal with two kinds of canned milk in most recipes. Sweetened Condensed Milk which is used in pies, salads, etc. and is very sweet. The second kind is evaporated milk which is not sweet and is also used in some pies (pumpkin), homemade ice cream, etc. However, the kind of milk Alyson needed was the kind you drink and keep in your refrigerator. Many recipes call for one or 1/2 soup cans of milk. This means to fill the soup can with the amount of milk required after you have taken the soup out of the can and added it to your recipe.

This can be a little confusing to a beginning cook, so if you have any questions about ingredients in a recipe ask your mother, or give me a call (with your parents permission) at 407-723-5111.

Kevin and Colleen Browning
3 years old and 2 years old

Breakfast

Elizabeth Guth

Breakfast

Cinnamon Sugar Toast

1 slice bread
1 teaspoon margarine
2 Tablespoons white sugar
1 teaspoon cinnamon

Toast bread the way you like it and butter it. Mix sugar and cinnamon in small dish and sprinkle lightly over toast. Serve while it is still warm.

(Contributed by Richard and Dee Burner)

(Another good way to make cinnamon toast is to butter your bread, then sprinkle on mixed cinnamon and sugar. Bake in a 350 degree oven until lightly brown.)

Cheese Toast

Bread
Cheese slices

Place one or two slices of bread (for each person) on a baking sheet. Place one slice of cheese on top of each slice of bread. Bake in 350 degree oven until cheese begins to melt. Serve at once. (Remove Cheese Toast from baking sheet with a wide spatula.)

Cheese Toast is great with soup, or delicious for a quick breakfast.

Oatmeal with Raisins

This is a good breakfast food, and very easy to fix.

1/4 cup instant oatmeal
3/4 cup water
1/4 cup raisins
1 Tablespoon brown sugar

Combine all ingredients, put on burner of stove and cook on medium heat for 1-2 minutes, stirring occasionally. Remove pot from burner, add brown sugar to taste, pour into your bowl and eat.

Toast or bagels are great with this. Add a glass of milk or orange juice and you are ready for a day at school, or play.

Kitchen Help

Great idea from Charlene Mathews — Keep a bottom drawer full of measuring spoons, cups, pot, pans, measuring cups, etc. for the youngest children to play with while you are cooking.

Also good idea to include small plastic containers with tops, plastic cups, forks and spoons. Anything they can safely take apart and put back together again. JB

Green Eggs and Ham

1 large egg
1 slice ham
Green food coloring

Break egg open and place in small bowl. Add several drops of green food coloring. Take a fork and mix until it is nice and green. Add another drop of green food coloring if it isn't green enough for you.

Place slice of ham in a frying pan and slowly cook until done. Just before ham is done, spray a small teflon frying pan with vegetable spray. Place on a small burner and turn to medium heat. When hot, add egg and stir several times until no longer runny, or as done as you like it. Place on a plate with your ham. Now enjoy eating your Green Eggs and Ham!

(Contributed by Peggy Pifer. The children in her class enjoy eating Green Eggs and Ham each year.)

Raisin Bran Muffins

1 1/4 cups all-purpose flour
3 teaspoons baking powder
1/2 teaspoon salt
1/2 cup sugar
1 1/4 cups milk
3 cups raisin bran
1 egg
1/3 cup vegetable oil
3/4 cup raisins

Stir together flour, baking powder, salt and sugar; set aside. Stir milk and raisin bran together in a large bowl and let it stand for 2 minutes. Add egg and vegetable oil to raisin bran and milk, stirring well to combine. Add raisins. Add dry ingredients to raisin bran mixture, stirring only until mixed. Spoon batter into 12 greased muffin cups. Bake in 400 degree oven for 25 minutes or until golden brown.

Happy Face Milk

1 glass of milk
Few drops of food coloring of your choice

Use food coloring in milk for the child who doesn't want to drink milk, or just for the fun of it! My kids always thought it was great.

What you do is what you believe, all the rest is just talk! (Think about what this says!)

Piglets in a Blanket

5 good grade hot dogs
1 package refrigerator biscuits

Cut hot dogs into halves. Flatten each biscuit and place the half hot dog in center of biscuit. Fold biscuit over in half-moon shape and pinch edges together. Bake in 450 degree oven for 10-12 minutes. A strip of cheese can be enclosed in blanket with hot dog, or place on top, if desired. Makes 10.

Sausage Balls

2 cups biscuit baking mix
1 pound lean pork sausage
8-10 ounces sharp Cheddar cheese, grated

Combine all ingredients in a large bowl. Mix thoroughly (you may have to use your hand, so be very sure to wash them first), then roll in balls the size of a small walnut. Place on a cookie sheet, not touching each other, and freeze. When frozen, place in a freezer bag and return to the freezer until about 20 minutes before serving. Bake at 350 degrees for 20 minutes. Serve hot.

(This is a wonderful, very popular appetizer, but my kids have always loved having them for breakfast. Just keep a batch in the freezer and remove the needed amount, then bake and eat!)

Lunch (Dinner)

Nicholas Guth

Lunch (Dinner)

Pink Rabbit Soup

1 can tomato soup
1 soup can milk
Popped Popcorn

Pour the tomato soup and the soup can of milk into a small pot. Place on burner and turn on heat to medium. When it begins to get a little hot, turn heat to low. Stir once in a while, and do not boil.

Pop your popcorn while the soup is heating.

Take a 1 cup measuring cup and divide the Pink Rabbit Soup into two bowls. Put one or two handsful of popped popcorn on top. Eat while it is warm...you will love it!

Invite your dad to share your lunch.

Quick and Yummy Soup

1 can Cream of Mushroom soup
1 can Cream of Asparagus soup
1 soup can of milk
1 can of tuna fish (in water), drained

Pour the mushroom soup, asparagus soup and the milk into a medium pot. Stir until it is all mixed well. Place the opened tuna fish in a strainer until the water is drained out, then add it to the soup in the pot. Place the pot on the stove burner.

Turn the burner on the stove to medium heat, stir a little, then turn the burner to low so that it won't burn the soup.

Get two soup bowls, dip out the soup with a measuring cup, place on the kitchen table, call your mom to lunch and enjoy!

Snack Pizzas

1 package English muffins
1 jar pizza sauce
Pepperoni slices
Mozzarella cheese, grated

Split English muffins into halves. Place on cookie sheet with cut side up. Top each half with 1 tablespoon of pizza sauce, pepperoni slices, and lots of cheese. Bake in 400 degree oven for 5 minutes or until cheese is melted.

Bacon, Lettuce and Tomato (Sandwich)

4 slices bacon, fried crisp
3 slices tomato
2 crisp lettuce leaves
2 slices of your favorite bread
1 slice cheese (optional)
Mayonnaise

Place mayonnaise on top sides of both pieces of bread. Crisp lettuce on bottom, then tomato slice and last 4 slices of bacon. Top with second slice of bread and enjoy! A slice of cheese on top of your warm bacon is a nice addition.

(Place four slices of bacon in frying pan, turn heat to medium. As bacon begins to sizzle, take a fork with sharp points and turn bacon over so it can cook on other side. Do this several times until bacon is nice and brown. Take out of frying pan with fork and place on several layers of paper towels so that all the grease can be absorbed by paper towel.)

Bacon can also be cooked in microwave. Your parents will have to show you how to use your particular microwave.

Tuna Fish Salad

1 can tuna, (packed in water), drained (Tuna packed in oil tastes best, but has many more calories)
1/4 small onion, finely chopped
2 stalks celery, finely chopped
1/4 cup sweet pickles, finely chopped
1/4 cup red bell pepper, finely chopped
1/4 cup mayonnaise, or to taste
2 slices tomato
1 lettuce leaf

Combine tuna, onion, celery, pickles, bell pepper and mayonnaise and mix well. Place desired amount on whole wheat, rye or white bread. Add lettuce leaf and tomato. Cut in half and serve on pretty plate with seedless grapes in 1/4 cantaloupe. (Serve with chips if you don't eat grapes and cantaloupe.)

Grilled Cheese

2 slices of your favorite bread
2 slices of Cheddar cheese
Mayonnaise
Margarine

Put mayonnaise on one side of each piece of bread. Place cheese slices on one side then cover with second slice of bread. Cover outer sides of both slices with margarine. Place in skillet to brown lightly then carefully flip over and brown second side. Eat while hot.

(Sliced "hunk" cheese is also great on a grilled cheese sandwich.)

Say "thank-you" often!

Grilled Ham and Cheese (Sandwich)

Grilled Ham and Cheese is the same as Grilled Cheese except for the slice of ham that is added. Grilled Ham and Cheese is a delicious sandwich!

Peanut Butter Sandwiches

Peanut butter sandwiches are great for children and adults. Give these a try!

1. **Peanut Butter and Dill Pickles**

   Crunchy or Smooth Peanut butter on white bread with thick slices of dill pickles. Yum! (My dad and I had one of these almost every night for a snack before bedtime. I still love them.)

2. **Peanut Butter and Tomato Slices**

   Crunchy or Smooth Peanut butter on white or whole wheat bread with thick tomato slices. (I have never tried this one, but my friend Bev Shannon vows it is delicious.)

3. **Peanut Butter and Bananas**

   Same as above except use sliced, ripe bananas instead of tomatoes.

4. **There are many other variations of Peanut Butter Sandwiches. Some are too questionable to print here. However, be imaginative and create your own favorite.**

Banana Dog

1 fresh hot dog bun
1 Tablespoon peanut butter
1 Tablespoon honey
1 small banana, peeled

Spread peanut butter over inside of hot dog bun, then spread thin layer of honey over peanut butter. Place banana inside, eat and enjoy!

(Contributed by Peggy Pifer)

Surprise Hamburgers or Cheeseburgers

Ground beef
Cheese slices
Olive slices
Cherries
Pickles

Make two thin burger patties about the same size. On top of 1 patty, place cheese slice, olive slices, cherries, pickles or whatever you like; then place a second patty on top of this and pinch edges of both burgers together to seal. Then fry, grill or bake as usual.

Everyone loves to find the surprise you put inside the burger!

Cheese Dogs

2-4 good grade hot dogs
Cheese slices or hunk of cheese

Slice hot dogs lengthwise about 3/4 of the way through. Cut a length of cheese to fit and place in the cut hot dog.

Place on a baking sheet and bake in 325 degree oven for 5-10 minutes or until cheese has melted. Serve with or without a hot dog bun.

What you do is what you believe,
all the rest is JUST TALK!

Colleen's Special Sandwiches

My sister, Colleen Barton, loaded lunch boxes with special shaped sandwiches for her children and her husband...she still makes these for Dennis (her husband).

Peanut butter and jelly sandwiches shaped like hearts, pumpkins, witches, bunnies, etc. Something special for each holiday. Needless to say, those lunch boxes always come home empty!

Sue's Open Face Sandwiches

1 slice bread
1 slice cheese
1 slice tomato
3 slices bacon, fried crisp

Put mayonnaise on bread, then add remaining ingredients. Good!

Black Cow

1 glass or mug half full of root beer
2 scoops vanilla ice cream

Pour cold root beer into a glass or mug to half full. Gently spoon in vanilla ice cream.

(Do this in a place where a spill or overflow won't be a disaster for you or your mom.)

(Contributed by Dee Burner as a favorite of her grandfather, Adolf Shaffer; now the whole family likes it.)

Lisa's Polish Soup

Lisa Gagnon brought this recipe home from her Brownie Girl Scout leader. Her leader was cooking the soup for supper for her family, it smelled so good that Lisa asked for a taste, then demanded the recipe to take home to her mother. It is still a family favorite!

1 pound Kielbasa (sausage), sliced
2 cups sliced celery with leaves
2 cups pared (cleaned) and sliced carrots
1/2 teaspoon leaves
3 cups peeled potatoes, cut into tiny cubes
1 Tablespoon instant beef bouillon
1 cup onions, finely chopped
4 cups cabbage, shredded
1 bay leaf
2 Tablespoons vinegar
6 1/2 cups water
1 1/2 teaspoons salt

In a dutch oven, or large heavy pot, cook Kielbasa sausage, onion and celery until tender. Add remaining ingredients except potatoes. Bring to a boil, then turn heat down to lowest heat and cook covered for 1 1/2 hours. Carefully add potatoes and cook covered for 20 minutes more. Serve with a small unsliced loaf of pumpernickel bread which has been warmed in the oven or bread you make yourself.

Bunny Salad

1/2 pear
2 raisins (eyes)
1 red candy (nose)
2 almond slices (ears)
1 teaspoon cottage cheese (tail)
1 lettuce leaf

Place lettuce leaf on salad plate. Put flat side of pear on lettuce leaf. Use narrow end of pear to make face. Raisins on both sides to form eyes, red candy for the nose, and almond slices for the ears. Form the cottage cheese into a small ball for the tail. Be creative!

Pizzas "Almost from Scratch"

1 box of pizza mix
Pepperoni slices
Ground beef, browned in skillet (drain off any grease)
Onions
Bell pepper
1/2 cup grated cheese

Combine crust according to mix directions. Coat your hands with vegetable oil, spreading dough in pizza pan as thin as possible...use your fingers. If you tear the crust, just stick it back together again. Bake crust in 350 degree oven for 5 minutes. Remove pan from oven and then carefully put on pizza sauce, toppings of your choice and sprinkle with grated cheese. Return to oven for 5 minutes. Put pizza pan on unheated burner top and cut into slices. (Ask an adult to help with this part if you need help.)

(Contributed by Gee Gee Wood's married daughters Donna, Diane and Denise as a favorite childhood memory.)

From Peggy Gagnon —

We have always held hands when we say grace and it has led to some interesting stories. My favorite is my sister-in-love Kathy's niece Christine who lives in Tampa. Her family was at a Little League Dinner at a Pizza Hut and Christine (age 4) was invited by another family to sit with them for dinner. When the Pizza was delivered, the family started to eat. Christine said loudly "Aren't you going to say a prayer?" They quickly asked Christine to say a prayer. Christine then said, "We have to hold hands." They held hands. At this point every eye was on them and Christine yelled to the entire crowd, "Aren't you going to hold hands?" Every one in the Pizza Hut held hands while Christine prayed. Out of the mouths of babes! It's amazing how a little seed can grow!

Dinner (Supper)

Thomas Guth

Dinner (Supper)

Ginny's Quick Rolls

2 cups self rising flour
1 cup milk
4 Tablespoons real mayonnaise

Mix all ingredients together. Fill greased muffin tins about 3/4 full. Bake at 400 degrees for 12-14 minutes. Yield: 12 rolls.

Baked Steak

1 large, thick, lean round steak (or 4-6 cube steaks)
1 envelope dried onion soup mix
1 can Cream of Mushroom soup
1 Tablespoon soy sauce

Place steak in a 9 x 13 inch baking dish. Sprinkle dried onion soup mix over steak. Mix soup and soy sauce, then spread over top of steak. Cover baking dish with foil.

Bake in 325 degree oven for 1 hour. Serve with rice, toss salad and a roll.

(Do not add salt.)

Jenny's Meatloaf Rings with Cheesy Potatoes

When it was Jenny Gagnon's turn to cook,
her artistic side took over. This is one of hers!

1 pound ground beef
1 pound ground turkey
1 egg
3/4 cup oatmeal
1 teaspoon instant beef bouillon
2 teaspoons horseradish
1/2 cup milk
1 1/2 teaspoons salt
1/2 cup chopped onion

Mix all ingredients (you may have to use CLEAN fingers to mix meatloaf).

Divide the meatloaf mixture into 8 equal balls. On an ungreased jelly roll pan, flatten the rings with your hand and, using your thumb, make a big hole in the center of each one so the ring is shaped like a doughnut. Bake at 350 degrees for 35 minutes. About 10 minutes before the rings are done, make the Cheesy Potatoes (see page 52 for recipe).

Cheesy Potatoes

2 2/3 cups instant mashed potatoes
2/3 cup milk
1 teaspoon salt
2 2/3 cups water
4 Tablespoons margarine
1/3 cup shredded Cheddar cheese

Heat the water, milk, salt and margarine until margarine has melted. Stir in potatoes and mix well. Add cheese and stir until cheese has melted.

When Meatloaf Rings are done, put one on each serving plate and fill center with Cheesy Potatoes. (See page 51 for Meatloaf Rings' recipe.)

Oven Potatoes (Baked Slices)

3 large baking potatoes

Wash and dry potatoes. Wrap in foil and bake in 450 degree oven for 1 hour, or stick a hole in potatoes and bake in microwave for 10 minutes on high.

Spray teflon baking sheet with vegetable spray. Slice baked potatoes into 1/4 inch rounds and place in single layer on baking sheet. Salt lightly with regular or seasoned salt. Bake in 350 degree oven for about 30 minutes, turning over each slice two or three times. Eat Hot!

Gagnon's Corn Sticks

Start kids cooking early and they'll be creative in the kitchen. This is one that's a great starter recipe and tastes like it was a lot of work!

2 cups biscuit baking mix
1 stick margarine
1 small can creamed corn
Flour

Mix biscuit baking mix and corn together. Sprinkle cutting board with flour and roll out dough. Cut into strips. Roll strips in flour. Melt 1 stick margarine on a cookie sheet lined with foil. Roll floured strips in margarine and bake at 350 degrees for 10 to 15 minutes (depending on how thick you make them) or until done.

Frozen Salad

1 pint sour cream (Lite sour cream or yogurt is o.k.)
1/3 cup sugar
1 teaspoon lemon juice
1 cup pineapple tidbits, drained
1 or 2 bananas, sliced
1 small jar cherries, drained
1 cup seedless grapes, sliced into halves

Mix together sour cream, sugar and lemon juice, then add remaining ingredients and mix well. Place muffin liners in muffin tins and fill with salad mixture. Place in freezer. When frozen take from muffin tins (leave liners around salad) and place in a ziploc bag and return to freezer until 10 minutes before eating.

(Note — it is pretty to serve them on a small lettuce leaf or other green.)

Rice

1 cup rice
2 cups water
1/2 teaspoon salt

Combine rice, water and salt in 1 quart pot. Bring to a boil, stir well once with a fork (including bottom), put lid on, turn to lowest heat and let cook for 20 minutes. (Do not lift lid to check on rice, until done.)

Anyone can cook good rice. The secret is to stir once, then leave alone!

(Note — one (1) inch of stick of margarine can be added when beginning to cook, if desired.)

If you can't say something nice, don't say anything at all!

Green Bean Casserole

2 (16 ounce) cans whole green beans, drained
1 can Cream of Mushroom soup
1 large can French Fried Onions, crumbled

Combine all ingredients and place in a baking dish. Bake in 300 degree oven for 20 minutes. Serve hot.

Easy Meatloaf

2 pounds lean ground beef (Or 1 pound ground beef and 1 pound ground turkey)
1 small-medium onion, finely chopped
1 medium red or green bell pepper, finely chopped
2 stalks celery, finely chopped
1/3 cup instant or regular oatmeal
1 egg, slightly beaten
1 teaspoon Italian seasonings

Place all ingredients in a large mixing bowl. Wash your hands, then mix all ingredients together with your hands. Keep mixing until everything is completely mixed. Place all ingredients in an 8 x 8 inch baking dish and form into a loaf, or bake in a large loaf pan. Bake in a 350 degree oven for one hour.

Remove from oven, then drain off any fat. Be very careful because it is easy to burn yourself doing this.

(An optional treat is to pour a can of Tomato Sauce with Bits over the top and return to the oven for 5-10 minutes.)

Cheese and Macaroni

1 (8 ounce) package American cheese, cut into cubes
1 (8 ounce) package uncooked macaroni

Cook macaroni according to directions on package. Unless you are old enough, be sure to let your mom or dad drain off the boiling water when the macaroni is done. Add the cheese cubes and stir until it is melted.

You can put into a baking dish and bake in a 350 degree oven for 15-20 minutes or you can eat it as it is. Baked is best!

Chicken ala King

2 cans boneless white chicken chunks in broth
2 cans Cream of Mushroom soup
1/2 soup can of milk
1 small can of tiny English peas
Patty Shells

Combine chicken, soup, milk and peas and heat. Place in patty shells and serve.

(Contributed by Bonnie Sego)

Meatloaf in a Minute

2 pounds lean ground beef (Or 1 pound lean ground beef and 1 pound ground turkey)
2 Tablespoons Worcestershire sauce
1 envelope dried onion soup mix
1/3 cup oatmeal
1 egg, slightly beaten

Combine well with your clean hands, place in a baking dish and bake for approximately 1 hour at 350 degrees.

Easy Chicken and Rice

1 can Cream of Mushroom soup
1 soup can of milk
1/2 cup uncooked rice
1 can mushroom pieces, drained
1 package dried onion soup mix
8 pieces of chicken

Mix all ingredients together except chicken. Place in an 8 x 8 inch baking dish. Lay chicken pieces on top of rice mixture. Bake in a 350 degree oven for 1 hour.

Mexican Goulash

2 pounds lean ground beef
1 medium onion, finely chopped
1 can green beans, cut and drained
1 can whole corn, drained
1 can tomato sauce with bits
Fritos, crushed

Brown ground beef and onion together. Drain off any grease. Add beans, corn and tomato sauce with bits. Place in baking dish. Bake in a 300 degree oven for 30-45 minutes. Serve with Fritos or other corn chips to cover top of casserole.

E-Z Chicken Pot Pie

2 ready made pie crusts
1 can mixed vegetables
1 can Cream of Mushroom soup
1 can Cream of Potato soup
1/2 cup milk
1 1/2 cups cooked chicken cut into cubes

Put one crust into bottom of 1 quart casserole dish, bringing crust up the sides. Mix remaining ingredients thoroughly. Place in the casserole dish on top of the crust and top with other crust, seal the two crusts by pinching them together. Bake at 350 degrees for 45 minutes.

This recipe was contributed by Jane Davies and her little granddaughter Julia Davies — a favorite they enjoy making together.

Vegetable Soup

Do your own thing...and enjoy!

1 pound lean hamburger
2 cups beef bouillon
Salt and pepper
4 carrots, cleaned and thinly sliced
2 onions, cleaned and thinly diced
10 pods of peas, any kind
10 green beans, sliced into 1 inch sections
2 tomatoes, diced
2 potatoes, peeled and thinly diced
2 (any other vegetable that you like)

Place 1 pound lean hamburger in large, heavy skillet with 2 cups beef bouillon. Add salt and pepper and cover. Bring to a boil. Turn down heat and add diced vegetables. Be sure to have enough water to cover it all. Cook for 30 minutes, then serve.

(Peggy Pifer makes this with her kindergarten class. Each child brings in the vegetable they like and all are added to make vegetable soup. More beef and water will have to be added according to amount of vegetables added.)

Another special story from Peggy Gagnon —

Last Thanksgiving, Mother (Shirley Bartlett) made toll house cookies and no one knows what happened but they turned out like rocks. Mother is a great cook and she took all kinds of teasing from her Grandkids (and kids, too!) Imagine her wonderful face on Christmas morning when she unwrapped a beautiful box from Jenny (Peggy's daughter) and inside were two earrings and a pin...mothers own cookies that Jenny had varnished and made into jewelry.

Shirley says she is going to work this story into a lesson on humility.

(Shirley is a wonderful and gifted Sunday School Teacher for the Pairs and Spares Sunday School Class in Melbourne.)

Cakes

Justin Mast

Cakes

Great Quick Treat

1 cake mix
1 package flat bottom ice cream cones

Mix cake according to directions on box. Fill ice cream cones 1/2 to 3/4 full with cake batter. Microwave 2 1/2 minutes for each 4 cones. Top with icing, ice cream or cool whip.

(Another from Charlene Mathews)

Apple-Walnut Cake

1 can apple pie filling
2 cups all purpose flour
1 1/2 teaspoons baking soda
1 cup walnuts, chopped
1 teaspoon salt
2 eggs, beaten
2/3 cup vegetable oil
1 cup sugar
Sour Cream Topping

Spread pie filling in bottom of a 13 x 9 inch pan. Combine flour, sugar, baking soda and salt; sprinkle over pie filling. In mixing bowl, combine eggs, vanilla, oil and 3/4 cup walnuts, mix well. Pour over ingredients in baking pan. Stir only until blended well. Smooth batter evenly in pan. Bake at 350 degrees for 45 minutes. Remove from oven. Stick small holes in cake with a fork. Pour hot Sour Cream Topping over warm cake and sprinkle with 1/4 cup walnuts. Serve warm or cold, cut into squares.

Sour Cream Topping

1 cup sugar
1/2 cup sour cream
1/2 teaspoon baking soda

Combine ingredients in saucepan. Cook over low heat, stirring constantly, until mixture comes to a boil. Immediately remove from heat and pour over warm cake. (Watch carefully or topping will burn.)

Lemon Cake

1 box yellow cake mix
1 (3.4 ounce) box instant lemon pudding mix
3 eggs, beaten
1/4 cup vegetable oil
1 cup water

Put all ingredients into a large mixing bowl. Mix well with a beater. Pour into a lightly greased tube cake pan. Bake at 350 degrees for 45-50 minutes.

Let cool in pan for five minutes, then gently turn out onto serving dish.

Drizzle:
1 cup confectioners sugar
2 Tablespoons fresh lemon juice

Combine confectioners sugar and lemon juice. Take fork and stick some holes in the cake, then drizzle the combined sugar and lemon juice over top of cake.

(This cake is very easy to make...and good.)

Wacky Chocolate Cake

1 1/2 cups flour
1 cup sugar
1/4 cup cocoa
1 cup water
1 teaspoon baking soda
1 teaspoon vanilla
1/2 teaspoon salt
1 Tablespoon vinegar

Add ingredients in order listed. Mix well after each addition. Bake in 8 inch cake pan at 350 degrees for 30 minutes. Or bake in cup cake tins at 400 degrees for 12-15 minutes.

(The first cake Heather and Holly Mathews made alone.)

Dump Cake

1 can (21 ounces) cherry pie filling
1 can (20 ounces) crushed pineapple or pineapple tidbits and juice
1 package yellow or white cake mix
1 stick (1/2 cup) margarine or butter, melted

Spread cherry pie filling on bottom of 9 x 13 inch or slightly smaller baking pan. Pour pineapple on top of cherries, then layer cake mix on top of pineapple. Smooth out with back of a large spoon. Pour melted margarine over top of cake mix and slightly tilt pan so that margarine will spread over complete top. Bake in 350 degree oven for 35-45 minutes.

(Served warm with a scoop of vanilla ice cream on top is wonderful!)

One Pecan Holiday Coffee Cake

2 cups all purpose flour
3 teaspoons baking powder
1/2 teaspoon salt
4 Tablespoons melted butter or margarine
1 egg
1/2 pecan (shelled)
2/3 cup milk
1 can apple pie filling

Sift flour, baking powder and salt into a large mixing bowl. Add the margarine, egg and milk and mix until well blended. It will be a soft dough. Using a spoon, spread batter in a greased 9 x 13 inch pan. Be sure to hide a pecan half in the batter. Gently spoon the apple pie filling on top, pushing it into the dough. Add the topping and bake at 375 degrees for 30 minutes.

Topping

2 Tablespoons sugar
1 teaspoon cinnamon
4 Tablespoons butter or margarine, melted

Combine well and sprinkle over top of coffee cake just before baking.

(Person who finds pecan gets to open first gift, or give out gifts under tree.)

(Contributed by Carolyn Hazel)

Several months ago when my two year old granddaughter Rebecca was 22 months old and saying words, but not sentences, we had a special experience. While she was sitting in her high chair in my kitchen I placed a plate of food on her tray and told her to eat her supper. She smiled at me, held out both hands and said "God". I must have looked puzzled because she again said "God". I quickly took both her extended hands and asked if she wanted me to thank God for her food. She smiled at me and nodded "Yes", closed her eyes and bowed her head. Thank you God for her wonderful parents, and the blessing Rebecca is to me!

For generations mothers and children have baked together. So many people have wonderful memories of putting extra cake batter in a very small pan so that everyone could have a quick taste as soon as it was taken from the oven. Warm, loving, delicious memories!

Pies

Rebecca Mast

Pies

Easy Peach Pie

1 can condensed milk
Juice of 2 lemons
1 large container cool whip
2 cups fresh peaches, cut into bite size pieces
2 graham cracker pie crusts

Mix condensed milk, lemon juice, cool whip and fresh peaches together and pour into pie crusts. Place in refrigerator until ready to serve.

(Graham Cracker Pie Crust recipe on page 83)

Pumpkin Pie

1 (9 inch) pie shell
1 (16 ounce) can pumpkin
1 (14 ounce) can condensed milk
2 eggs, beaten
1 teaspoon cinnamon
1/2 teaspoon each ginger and nutmeg

Combine all ingredients and pour into pastry shell. Bake in a 425 degree oven for 15 minutes, then reduce heat to 350 degrees and bake for 30-35 minutes. Carefully remove from oven, cool slightly and eat. This is great with a heaping teaspoonful of cool whip on top of each slice.

(Be sure to store leftovers in the refrigerator.)

Brownie Chocolate Pie

1 stick margarine
1 cup white sugar
1/2 cup all purpose flour
2 Tablespoons cocoa
1 teaspoon vanilla
2 eggs

Melt margarine in saucepan on low heat, then add sugar and flour stirring well. Put the two eggs in a small bowl and beat them with a fork until they are creamy and yellow, then add to margarine mixture. Combine cocoa and vanilla, then add to other ingredients, stirring well. Pour into a pie plate with the inside covered with a thin layer of margarine. Bake in a 325 degree oven for 20-25 minutes. Eat while warm with ice cream on top, or serve at room temperature.

Lemon Pie

1 can condensed milk
1 (9 ounce) container cool whip, room temperature
1 small can (6 ounces) frozen lemonade, defrosted
1 baked pie shell

Mix milk and lemonade with mixer until smooth, then fold in cool whip. Pour into baked and cooled pie shell. Put in refrigerator until ready to eat.

Clay's "Yellow Pie"

1 prepared graham cracker crust

You can buy a prepared graham cracker crust from the grocery store or make your own. Making your own is the best, and it is very easy to do.

1 1/4 cups graham cracker crumbs
3 Tablespoons sugar
1/2 stick (1/4 cup) margarine, melted

Combine all three ingredients until well blended. Pour into 8-9 inch pie plate. With the back of a fork or spoon form a crust on the bottom and sides of the pie plate. Ask your mom to check it out for you the first time you make one.

Pie Filling

1 quart vanilla ice cream or frozen yogurt
1 teaspoon butternut flavoring
1 package instant vanilla pudding mix
2 squares semi-sweet baking chocolate
1 medium container cool whip

Mix ice cream, pudding mix and flavoring. Blend in 1/2 of the cool whip. Add 1 1/2 squares chocolate, grated. Pour into pie shell and frost with remaining cool whip. Decorate with remaining grated chocolate. Freeze until ready to serve.

(Contributed by Dee Dee Pannell and her grandson Clayton Townsend)

Note — I adapted this recipe so that my grandson Clayton could do most of it himself. I grate the chocolate and pour the mixture into the shell. He does the rest with a little help. He loves this dessert and calls it his "Yellow Pie".

Katie's Chocolate Pie

1 pie crust
1 can chocolate pie filling
1 small container cool whip

Bake pie crust in oven as directed on package. When cool, pour in chocolate pie filling. Cover top of pie with cool whip. Place in refrigerator until ready to serve.

(Contributed by my cousin, Jane McElyea and her little granddaughter Katie Jane McElyea)

Cookies

Virginia Brown
with great granddaughter, Rebecca Mast

Cookies

Lit'l Chef

Mommy, I'd like to help you cook,
But I know just what you'll say.
"I'm sorry, you're too little,
Please, dear, won't you move out of my way?"

If only you'll give me a chance, you'll see,
I'll really create a lot.
King size bon-bons, mud pies and such
Would surely hit the spot!

My hands, though small, can roll and pat,
A cookie dough just right.
My peanut butter and jelly cake,
It's sure to be moist and light.

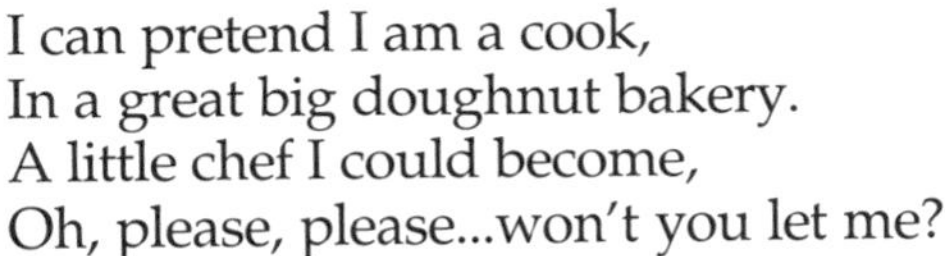

I can pretend I am a cook,
In a great big doughnut bakery.
A little chef I could become,
Oh, please, please...won't you let me?

I'm kinda short, I'll need a stool,
And an apron just my size.
Perhaps a spoon, some pots and pans,
For baking souffles and pies.

What's that? You say you will let me help?
I'll be a famous cook I bet.
I may spill a little, but be patient
God isn't finished with this lit'l chef yet!

A little flour here and there,
Or in our toes and hair,
Just add so much to our fun,
This "fun" that we will share.

So now I can cook, your lit'l chef,
I knew that you'd come through.
My first big cookie with chocolate chips,
Will be, Mommy, just for you!

*Written for **Kids at Work** by Julie Casper Clifton — October 1992*

Crispy Rice Bars

1 Tablespoon margarine
1/2 cup sugar
1/2 cup light corn syrup
1/2 cup peanut butter
2 1/4 cups crispy rice cereal

Get out an 8 x 8 x 2 inch baking dish and smear a light coat of margarine on the sides and bottom. You will probably have to use your hands to do this...make sure they are clean.

Put your margarine, sugar and corn syrup in a large pot, place on stove burner and slowly bring to a boil. As soon as it boils, take the pot off the hot burner and put it on one that has not been turned on. Stir in the peanut butter and mix well. Last add the rice cereal and stir until it is well mixed. Pour the rice bars into the baking dish and press down until it is even. Cut into squares with a table knife or the short end of a spatula. Eat!

(Be sure to save some for your mom and dad!)

(Donna, Diane and Denise Wood are so creative they made their Crispy Rice Bars into shapes of snowmen with gum drops or raisins for eyes — so put margarine on your hands and make your own shapes. Be creative!)

Hand Cookies

1/2 cup margarine
1/2 cup shortening
1 cup white sugar
2 eggs
1 teaspoon vanilla
2 1/2 cups all purpose flour
1 teaspoon baking powder

Cream (mix) together margarine and shortening, then gradually stir in sugar. Add eggs, one at a time, then add vanilla. Mix well.

Mix together flour, and baking powder. Gradually add flour mixture into margarine mixture, creaming well. Cover and refrigerate for one hour, or overnight. (This is necessary so that the dough will be easier to work with.)

Preheat oven to 400 degrees.

Sprinkle flour on the area where you will roll out cookie dough. Roll dough to about 1/8 inch thick. Place your hand (or someone else's) on the dough and cut out the form of your hand with a dull rounded-tip pastry or table knife. Place on baking sheet and reshape a little, if necessary. Bake for 5-7 minutes. Cool completely, then decorate.

Chocolate Chip Cookies

3 cups all-purpose flour
1 teaspoon baking soda
1 teaspoon salt
1 cup margarine
1 cup brown sugar
1 cup white sugar
2 eggs
1 teaspoon vanilla
3 cups (12 ounces) chocolate chips

Put margarine in a large mixing bowl and let come to room temperature. Mix flour, baking soda and salt together. Then add brown and white sugars, 2 eggs and vanilla to margarine and beat well. Add flour mixture to margarine mixture and mix well (it is stiff, but keep mixing). Add chocolate chips and mix into batter evenly.

Drop by tablespoonfuls onto cookie sheet and bake at 375 degrees for about 7-8 minutes. Take out of oven while they are still a little gooey in the center of cookie, and are light brown. Cookies will harden some as they cool.

(Contributed by my daughter, Tricia Mast)

Gingerbread Cookies (To cut out)

2 1/4 cups sugar
3/4 cup water
1/3 cup dark corn syrup or molasses
1 1/4 Tablespoons ground cinnamon
1 Tablespoon ground ginger
2 teaspoons ground cloves
1 cup and 2 Tablespoons margarine
1 Tablespoon water
8 cups all purpose flour
1 Tablespoon baking soda

Combine sugar, water, syrup and spices in medium saucepan. Cook over medium heat, stirring until sugar dissolves. Add margarine, stirring until melted. Dissolve soda in 1 tablespoon water; add to sugar mixture. Pour sugar mixture into a large bowl; gradually add flour, mixing well. Chill at least one hour in refrigerator.

Divide dough into 1/3's. Work with 1/3 of dough at a time while returning remaining batter to refrigerator until ready to use. Roll 1/3 of dough to 1/4-1/8 inch thickness on lightly floured surface. Cut with a 4 inch gingerbread man or woman cutter (or other shapes) and place on a lightly greased baking sheet. Bake at 350 degrees for 10-12 minutes. (Always stick your cookie cutter in flour before cutting the dough. This is so dough will not stick to cutter.) Cool one minute on pan then remove to wire racks and cool completely. Repeat with remaining dough.

(Contributed by Tricia, Justin and Rebecca Mast)

Richard's Favorite Toll House Cookies

4 1/2 cups all purpose flour
1 1/2 teaspoons salt
1 1/2 teaspoons baking soda
1 1/2 cups shortening
3/4 cup white sugar
1 1/2 cups dark brown sugar
3 eggs
1 1/2 teaspoons vanilla
1 (12 ounce) package semi-sweet chocolate chip morsels

Sift then measure flour. Add baking soda and salt and then sift three times; set aside. Cream shortening, then gradually add sugars, beating thoroughly after each addition. Beat eggs then add to mix and stir well. Add dry ingredients (flour, etc.) 1/3 at a time, beating until smooth each time. Add chocolate morsels and vanilla and mix well. Place about one teaspoonful in a ball shape on a cookie sheet, about 2 inches apart. Bake in 350 degree oven for 12-15 minutes. Remove from cookie sheet with wide spatula and cool on cooling rack. These cookies keep well in freezer.

(Tanya and Alyson Burner helped make these when they were small. As they got older they made them by themselves. Richard thinks these are wonderful with a glass of cold milk.)

School Lunches with Love

Include Iced Sugar Cookies in your child's lunch box. An Easter Egg shaped cookie at Easter, a pumpkin shaped cookie at Halloween or Thanksgiving, Valentine shaped cookie for Valentine's Day or his/her birthday, etc.

Iced Sugar Cookies

1/2 cup shortening
1/2 teaspoon salt
1 teaspoon grated lemon rind
1 cup sugar
1 egg, unbeaten
1 Tablespoon milk
2 cups all purpose flour
1 teaspoon baking powder
1/2 teaspoon baking soda

Preheat oven to 400 degrees. Mix together shortening, salt, lemon rind and sugar in medium mixing bowl. Add egg and milk to mixture and beat until smooth. Combine flour, baking powder, baking soda and mix well, then add to the shortening mixture. Mix well. Place rounded teaspoon full of dough onto greased baking sheet.

Spray bottom of glass with vegetable cooking oil, dip bottom of glass in sugar, then flatten each cookie. Sprinkle each cookie with a small amount of nutmeg. Bake 8-9 minutes or until light brown. Cool on your cookie rack. Makes about 3 dozen cookies.

Decorate!

(Contributed by Colleen Barton)

Good Cookies for Good Kids

Put 1/4 cup Sugar Cookie dough, (recipe page 93), into a small bowl. Add 2 tablespoons water and 2 tablespoons cocoa. Mix together until completely brown color.

Put remaining Sugar Cookie dough on baking sheet as directed in Sugar Cookie recipe. With a large toothpick make eyes, nose and mouth of chocolate dough. (Or you could use chocolate chips or raisins for the eyes and small red hot candies for the mouth.) Use the chocolate dough on a spoon to make hair.

Use your imagination. Be creative! Use dyed coconut for the hair (put coconut in a small paper bag with a few drops of food coloring and shake until coconut is desired color), decorative sprinkles for freckles, chocolate sprinkles for hair, etc.

No Bake Cookies

1 (6 ounce) package chocolate morsels
1 (6 ounce) package butterscotch morsels
1/2 cup crunchy peanut butter
4 cups rice krispie cereal

Put morsels and peanut butter in a heavy pot and turn burner to low heat. Slowly melt, then add rice krispies. Drop by teaspoonsful onto waxed or foil paper. Refrigerate, then enjoy!

Chocolate Oatmeal Cookies I

1/2 cup cocoa
1/2 cup margarine, melted
1 can condensed milk
2 eggs, beaten
2 teaspoons vanilla
1 1/2 cups instant oatmeal
1 cup biscuit baking mix
1 (6 ounce) package chocolate chips
1 (6 ounce) package peanut butter chips

Preheat oven to 350 degrees. Combine cocoa and margarine in a large mixing bowl and stir until well blended. Stir in remaining ingredients and mix well. Spray baking sheet with vegetable spray, then drop cookie batter by heaping teaspoonsful. Bake 7-8 minutes, but do not overbake. Cool for several minutes before removing from cookie sheet, then move with spatula to cooking rack.

Hello Dolly Cookies

1 stick margarine
1 cup graham cracker crumbs
1 cup pecans, finely chopped
1 cup raisins
1 cup coconut
1 (6 ounce) package chocolate chips
1 can sweetened condensed milk

Melt margarine in an 8 x 8 inch baking pan. Sprinkle graham cracker crumbs over margarine. Add a layer of pecans, then a layer of raisins, then a layer of chocolate chips and last a layer of coconut. Pour the condensed milk over top so that it covers all the coconut. Bake in a 350 degree oven for 30 minutes. Cool and cut into small squares. Yummy!

The wonderful smell of baking cookies! When Maria Casper, my youngest daughter's friend and a close neighbor, came to our house and I was baking cookies she always said, "Mrs. Browning, your house smells so happy!" This has always been a special memory for me.

Jiffy Peanut Butter Chews

1 can condensed milk
1/2 cup peanut butter
2 cups graham cracker crumbs

Mix together until smooth. Drop by teaspoonsful 1 inch apart onto greased cookie sheet. Bake at 350 degrees for 15 minutes.

It is hard to stop a quarrel once it starts, so don't let it begin.

Proverbs 17:14

Nutty Ice Box Cookies

1 package pie crust mix
1 cup light brown sugar
1 egg, well beaten
1 teaspoon vanilla
1 cup chocolate chips

Mix sugar and dry pie crust mix. Add egg and vanilla and mix well. Stir in chocolate chips and mix well. Shape into a roll about 10 inches long (or make two (2) shorter ones). Chill in refrigerator for several hours, then slice about 1/4 inch thick. Bake on an ungreased cookie sheet for 8-10 minutes at 375 degrees. (They can also be wrapped in foil and frozen until ready to bake.)

My grandmother, Lizzie Brown, gave me this recipe at least 30 years ago, and it is still a favorite.

Peanut Butter Fudgies (No Bake)

1/3 cup cold mashed potatoes
1/4 cup peanut butter
2 cups confectioners sugar
1/4 cup powdered milk
2 heaping Tablespoons chocolate chips

Put mashed potatoes and peanut butter in mixing bowl and mix well. Add confectioners sugar, powdered milk and chocolate chips. Mix well. Put a teaspoonful in your hand and roll into a ball. Add more powdered milk if too sticky.

(Contributed by Connie Helsky)

Know that man shall not live by bread alone; but man lives by every word that proceeds from the mouth of the Lord.

Deuteronomy 8:3

"Boiled Cookies"

1 stick margarine
1/2 cup milk
1/2 cup cocoa
1 1/2 cups sugar
1 teaspoon vanilla
1/2 cup crunchy peanut butter
3 cups oatmeal
1 cup coconut

Microwave the margarine on "high" for 1 minute. Add milk, cocoa, and sugar and microwave on "high" for 5-6 minutes. Stir once or twice, then add remaining ingredients. Mix well. Drop onto waxed paper and cool. Makes several dozen cookies.

(Charlene Mathews contributed this recipe and she says you can put in refrigerator or freezer to harden quickly on a hot, humid day.)

Chocolate Oatmeal Cookies II

1/2 cup milk
2 cups sugar
1 stick margarine (1/4 cup)
6 Tablespoons cocoa
1 teaspoon vanilla
3 cups instant oatmeal

Put milk, sugar, margarine and cocoa in a saucepan. Turn burner to medium high heat, and bring ingredients to a boil. Boil and stir for 1 1/2 minutes. Add vanilla and oatmeal, stir well then let cool for five minutes. Drop by teaspoonsful onto waxed or foil paper and let set until firm.

Peanut Blossoms

1 (14 ounce) can sweetened condensed milk
3/4 cup peanut butter
2 cups biscuit mix
1 teaspoon vanilla
1/2 cup sugar
1 large bag chocolate kisses

Preheat oven to 375 degrees. Mix condensed milk and peanut butter until smooth. Add biscuit mix and vanilla; mix well. Shape into 1 inch balls. Roll each ball in sugar until the ball is completely covered with sugar. Place 2 inches apart on cookie sheet. Bake 6-8 minutes. Remove from oven and immediately press a chocolate candy kiss in center of each ball. Good!

(While cookies are baking unwrap your candy kisses and have ready to place in center of hot cookie.)

Cookies to Share

I'd like to bake some cookies
 I told my Mom one day.
I'd rather bake the cookies
 Than go outside and play.

For I've a friend and neighbor
 Who's getting kinda old
She isn't feeling very well
 Or, that's what I've been told.

I'll bet she'd love some cookies
 So I'll take them in a while
I'll hold her hand and hug her,
 And then I'm sure she'll smile.

Written for ***Kids at Work*** *by Carolyn Hazel '92*

Peggy's Rainbow Cookies

1 cup margarine
3/4 cup white sugar
3/4 cup brown sugar
2 eggs
1 teaspoon vanilla
3 cups all-purpose flour
1/2 teaspoon baking soda
1/2 teaspoon salt
Red, yellow, green and blue food coloring

Put margarine and sugar into bowl and stir until creamy. Add eggs one at a time, stirring until mixed well before adding another. Add vanilla and stir.

Mix flour, baking soda and salt together, then gradually add to margarine mixture. Mix well. Divide dough into four (4) parts. Add several drops of food coloring to each part of dough, mix until color you want.

On waxed paper, or foil, mold each color of dough into a strip 4 inches long by 1/4 inch wide. Stack the rainbow strips on top of one another and press just hard enough to get them to stick together. Put in refrigerator for one hour or longer.

Slice 1/4 inch thick section and gently curve into an arch (like a rainbow). Bake on any ungreased cookie sheet for 7 minutes. Bake in 375 degree oven.

Pecan Bars

1 1/2 sticks margarine
2 cups firmly-packed light brown sugar
2 eggs
1 cup all-purpose flour
1 cup chopped pecans
Powdered sugar

Melt margarine, then add brown sugar. Add eggs to sugar mixture and beat a little. Add flour and pecans. Bake in a 12 x 9 x 2 inch baking pan (not glass) for 25 minutes at 350 degrees. Remove from oven and sprinkle with powdered sugar. Cool, then cut into bars.

(These are very easy to make and are really delicious. My 11 year old granddaughter, Elizabeth, has been making these for years!)

Peanut Butter Crunchies

1 cup clear karo syrup
1/2 cup sugar
12 ounces crunchy peanut butter
6 cups corn flakes

Heat karo syrup and sugar until it boils.* Pour into bowl, add peanut butter and mix well. Add corn flakes and stir until well mixed. Drop by spoonful on waxed paper.

*Syrup and sugar can be heated to a boil in the microwave.

(Merilee Clifton and her son, Scott, made these when he was a child. Scott is now grown, and still loves them!)

Peanut Butter with Chocolate Chip Cookies

1 3/4 cups all purpose flour
1/2 cup white sugar
1/2 cup brown sugar, firmly packed
1 teaspoon baking soda
1/2 teaspoon salt
1/2 cup margarine or solid shortening
1 teaspoon vanilla
1/2 cup smooth peanut butter
1 egg
2 Tablespoons milk
2 cups chocolate chips

Combine shortening or margarine with sugars and mix well. Add peanut butter, egg, milk and vanilla and beat well. Mix flour, baking soda and salt together. Add this to sugar mixture and blend well. Stir in chocolate chips. Put dough into plastic container and refrigerate for about 2 hours.

Remove from refrigerator and shape into medium sized balls (walnut size). Roll balls in additional sugar in a small, shallow bowl. Place balls on ungreased cookie sheets (about 12 to a large cookie sheet).

Bake at 375 degrees for about 10 minutes or until lightly browned.

(Contributed by Tricia Mast)

Chocolate Peanut Butter Squares

1 cup smooth peanut butter
1 cup semi-sweet chocolate chips
1/2 cup margarine (1 stick) cut into small pieces
1 bag (10 1/2 ounces) mini-marshmallows
2 cups crisp rice cereal

Spray 8 inch square pan with vegetable spray. Set aside. Put peanut butter, chocolate chips and margarine in a 3 quart microwave safe bowl. Microwave uncovered on high for 2 to 2 1/2 minutes until margarine melts and chocolate chips look glossy and soft, but still keep their shape. Stir until smooth. Stir in marshmallows and microwave on high for 45-60 seconds (marshmallows will be slightly melted). Stir to mix all ingredients together.

Stir in cereal until well mixed. Using a large spoon scrape mixture into prepared pan. Spread evenly with the back of your large spoon or with slightly wet fingers (make sure mixture isn't too hot to touch). Pat evenly in pan.

Put in refrigerator until firm. Cut into squares and keep refrigerator in tupperware to keep from being too sticky. Remove from refrigerator when ready to eat.

(Contributed by my daughter, Tricia Mast)

Peanut Butter Cookies

1 (14 ounce) can sweetened condensed milk
3/4 cup peanut butter (smooth or crunchy)
2 cups biscuit mix
1 teaspoon vanilla
1/4 cup sugar
IDEA! — 1 cup chocolate chips added to batter is great!

Preheat oven to 375 degrees (turn dial to 375 degrees then turn oven on).

In a large mixing bowl beat condensed milk and peanut butter until smooth. Add biscuit mix and vanilla and mix well. Take a teaspoon and put a large teaspoonful of the cookie dough in your hand and roll it around until it is fairly smooth (no big lumps). Put the 1/4 cup sugar in a little dish and roll the ball of cookie dough until it is covered with sugar. Place the cookie on a cookie sheet and press down lightly (just a little) with a fork. Place the cookies about two inches apart on the cookie sheet. (This is two inches:
——————————)
Place the cookie sheet in the oven on the top shelf and bake for 6-8 minutes or until they are lightly browned (do not overbake). Take from cookie sheet and place on cooling rack. Cool, then store in ziploc bags.

Desserts, Candy & Breads

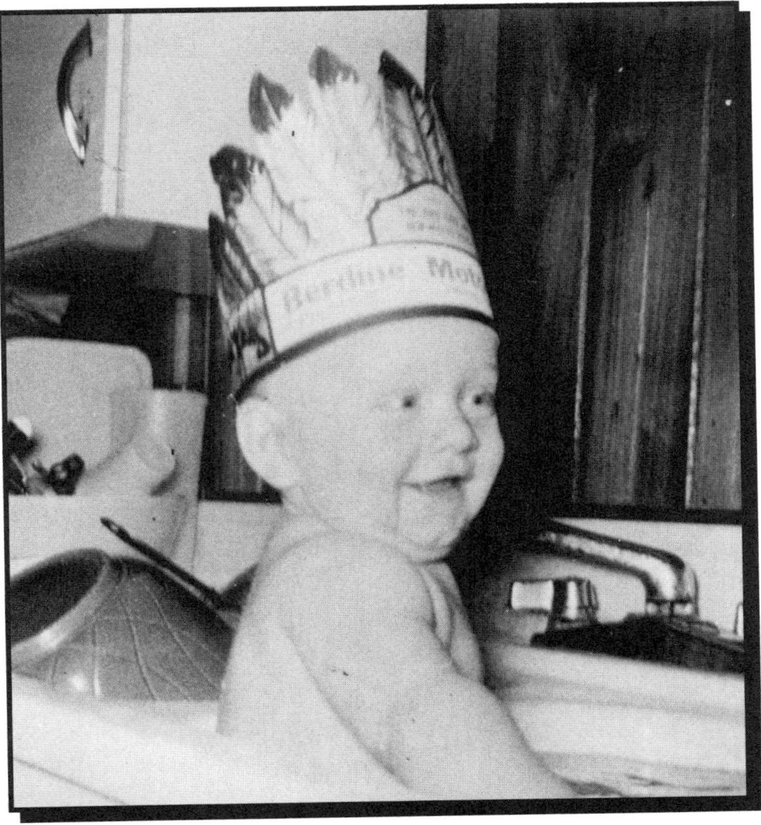

All our children and grandchildren have loved taking a bath in the kitchen sink.

Desserts, Candy & Breads

Gorp

Sugar coated chocolate candy (any kind)
Spanish peanuts
Raisins
Small pretzels

Mix all together in a large mixing bowl then put just enough for one person in a small ziploc bag. Use as a snack when you travel or in your school lunch. (Maybe you could give dad one as a surprise in his lunch!)

S'Mores

1 box Graham Crackers
1 bag of large marshmallows
1 chocolate bar per person

Break a graham cracker into a square (break large crackers in half). Place 2 squares on each persons plate. Take wrapper off chocolate bar and break in half. Put 1/2 of chocolate bar on each cracker half. Place one or two large marshmallows on a long skewer and roast over coals until marshmallow is light brown on outside and gooey inside. Quickly place roaster marshmallow on chocolate bar, cover with another cracker and gently mash together. Heat from marshmallows will melt chocolate bar and you have a delicious dessert.

S'Mores are great any time you have some red hot coals whether on your outdoor grill, a bonfire on the beach, a cookout in the park, or over the coals in your fireplace. (Be sure to check with Mom and Dad before you try this in your home.)

Marshmallows can be cooked on skewers, an unwound clothes hanger, a dowel stick, a palmetto branch that can be cut and shaped to fit your marshmallows. (Just be sure that whatever you use is clean and non-poisonous.)

This is a great time to sit around and do some "Gang" singing with your family or friends. No one has to be a great singer — just hum, clap your hands, or stomp your feet to the music. Have fun!

Peggy's Trail Mix

You will need:
Small round cereal
Pretzel sticks
Raisins
Fish Crackers
Chocolate chips
Ziploc bag

1. Wash and dry hands.

2. Count out and put in ziploc bag:
   10 small round cereal
   9 pretzel sticks
   8 raisins
   7 fish crackers
   6 chocolate chips

3. Zip the bag and shake.

4. Enjoy it, partner.

5. Clean up.

This is great to take on a nature walk. It is also fun to put in an ice cream cone, and you can just eat the cone, too.

(Kindergarten teacher Peggy Pifer contributed this fun idea)

Rice Pudding

As a kid, I was always happy when my mother made Rice Pudding. Mother always said she made it because there was leftover rice and she didn't want to waste it. But looking back, it seems she always made extra rice so we could have Rice Pudding.

2 cups cooked rice
1 cup milk
1 egg, beaten
1/2 cup sugar or to taste
1 teaspoon vanilla

Combine all ingredients and mix well. Put in a small baking dish. Place in 350 degree oven and bake for 25-30 minutes. Do not let it dry out.

Jon's Rice Pudding

This is one of Jon Gagnon's all time favorites!

1/2 cup rice
1 cup water
1 quart milk
4 Tablespoons margarine
3 eggs
1/2 cup sugar
1 cup raisins
1/2 teaspoon vanilla
3 Tablespoons sugar
1 Tablespoon cinnamon

In a large pot bring water to boil, then add rice. DON'T STIR! Cover and cook for 7 minutes. Add milk and margarine. Stir to loosen rice from bottom of pan. Bring to a boil, cover and cook on lowest heat for 1 hour. In a small bowl, beat eggs. Add sugar, raisins and vanilla. Pour into rice. Stir slowly until rice starts to thicken. Serve hot, warm or cold with sugar and cinnamon sprinkled on top.

Chocolate Syrup

1 1/2 cups white sugar
3/4 cup unsweetened cocoa
1 cup hot water
Dash of salt
2 teaspoons vanilla

Combine sugar, cocoa and salt in a medium saucepan. Gradually stir in water, blending until mixture is smooth. Cook over medium heat, stirring constantly, until mixture boils. Boil and stir for 3 minutes. Remove from heat and add vanilla, mix well. Cool a little then put into a storage container. Refrigerate.

(For chocolate milk add 2 tablespoons chocolate syrup to a glass of cold milk, stir well. Good also to pour over ice cream.)

(Contributed by my daughter, Tricia Mast)

Pretty is as pretty does.

Peanut Butter Pudding

1 package (4 serving size) vanilla pudding mix
2 cups milk
1/2 cup crunchy peanut butter

Pour milk into mixing bowl. Add peanut butter and pudding mix. Beat slowly just until well mixed...about 1-2 minutes. Pour into serving bowls and let stand to set.

Fun for the Whole Family — Burner's Christmas Candy

1 3/4 cups granulated sugar
1/2 cup white Karo syrup
1/2 cup water
1/2 teaspoon oil flavoring
Food coloring
Powdered sugar

Mix sugar, syrup and water. Bring to boil and cook to 300 degrees (hard crack), stirring occasionally. Remove from heat, add flavoring and food coloring (10 to 20 drops). Stir well and pour quickly on smooth surface which has been well coated with powdered sugar. Sift more powdered sugar on top. Let set until it can be cut into pieces without sticking to scissors or without making long, thin strings. Cut around the edges. Cut fast! Shake off excess sugar in colander.

Some notes: The smooth surface can be a cutting board or formica counter top. It must be able to stand some heat. In addition to keeping the candy from sticking, the powdered sugar provides some thermal protection for the surface. The powdered sugar on top keeps it from cooking too fast. It will get to a cutting consistency around the edges while it is still too fluid in the middle. If it gets to cool, it will shatter when you try to cut it. If you are making a number of batches, shake the powdered sugar off the candy with a colander, causing the sugar to drop in a smooth flat pattern on the cutting surface, so it will be ready for the next batch. Watch the candy closely when it gets near 300 degrees; the last few degrees go very fast and the difference between hard crack and scorch is not much time. We seem always to scorch one batch.

The vapors that rise from the candy when the oil flavoring is added will provide a very nice long-lasting aroma in the kitchen. A word of caution: if anyone is allergic or sensitive to one of the flavors used, they should leave the room when the flavoring is being stirred in. Following are the flavors by color we last used.

(Continued on page 121)

Burner's Christmas Candy Flavors

Purple .... Anise
Light Yellow-Green .... Apple
Blue .... Clove
Brown .... English Toffee
Yellow................................. Lemon
Red .... Peppermint
Clear or Milky White .... Pina Colada
Orange .... Sassafras
Pink .... Watermelon
Green .... Wintergreen

When Tanya and Alyson were small, they looked forward to the family time of cutting the candy together. They still do.

Mini-Cheesecakes

12 vanilla wafers, fresh and crisp
2 (8 ounce each) packages cream cheese, room temperature
1/2 cup white sugar
1 teaspoon vanilla
2 eggs, fresh

Place foil liners in mini muffin tins. The bottom of the muffin tin should be about the size of one vanilla wafer.

Mix cream cheese, sugar and vanilla until well blended. Add eggs, one at a time and mix well. Put one vanilla wafer in the bottom of each muffin liner. Pour cream cheese mixture over vanilla wafer, filling to just below the top. Bake in a 325 degree oven for 20-25 minutes.

Remove from oven, place pan on wire rack and let cool. Place in refrigerator (still in muffin pan, but covered) and chill. When ready to serve, remove from refrigerator and top each cheesecake with pie filling of your choice, jam, jelly or preserves, or shaved chocolate. Enjoy!

Cherry Cobbler

1 large can cherry pie filling
1 cup pecans, chopped or broken
1/2 package yellow cake mix
1 stick margarine, melted
Vanilla ice cream

Pour pie filling into an 8 x 8 x 2 inch baking dish, then sprinkle nuts over cherries. Cover with 1/2 package dry cake mix (that's right, just open up the package and pour half of it over the cherries) and pour melted margarine over top. Bake at 350 degrees for 25-30 minutes. Serve while hot with a scoop of vanilla ice cream on top.

This is a delicious dessert, and so very easy to make. (You don't have to tell everyone how easy it is to make!)

If you look for the bad in someone, you will surely find it. If you look for the good in someone, you will surely find that, too! So, always try to look for the good, and perhaps the bad will go away.

Burner's Sherbet

1 (3 ounce) package flavored gelatin
1 cup sugar
1 cup boiling water
1 quart whole milk

Dissolve gelatin and sugar in boiling water. Add milk, stirring thoroughly. Freeze.

There are at least two ways to freeze the sherbet. Take the dividers out of an ice tray and freeze until it becomes fairly firm. Scoop out into a bowl and beat with an egg beater until fluffy. Refreeze, then take out and beat again. It may have to be done a third time...you want it to be smooth and creamy.

Another (and easier) way to freeze is to churn it in an ice cream churn just as you would when you are making ice cream. If the churn makes five quarts you will have to double the recipe.

(This recipe came from Richard Burner who remembers making it at his grandmother, Mary Gillespie Burner's home in the 1940's. They froze it in ice trays and beat it with a manual eggbeater.)

Homemade Ice Cream

3 (12 ounce) cans evaporated milk
6-8 large eggs
2 cups white sugar
1 Tablespoon vanilla
2-3 cups fruit, cut up in small pieces or put through a blender
Suggested fruit: Strawberry, Peach, Blackberry, Banana, Pineapple, etc.

In large mixing bowl beat eggs for several minutes until light and fluffy. Slowly beat in sugar. Add 1 can evaporated milk at a time, beating well during and after each addition of milk. Last add vanilla and fresh fruit or frozen fruit. Canned crushed pineapple is also good.

(When our children were small we sometimes had "Surprise" ice cream. I usually combined several mashed bananas; a can of drained, crushed pineapple; a bottle of cherries, drained and a few chopped pecans. This was always a favorite.)

Grandma's Brown Bread

This is mixed in a mixing bowl with a spoon and plopped into a 9 x 5 inch bread pan. Very easy.

2 Tablespoons molasses
1 Tablespoon margarine or butter, soft
1/2 cup brown sugar
1 cup buttermilk
1 1/2 cups graham (whole wheat pastry) flour
1/2 cup all purpose flour
1 teaspoon baking soda
1 teaspoon salt
1/2 cup raisins

Put molasses and margarine in mixing bowl and stir together. Add sugar and stir well. Then add buttermilk and stir again. Mix together graham flour, white flour, baking soda, salt and raisins, then add to molasses mixture. Spray your bread pan with vegetable spray, then pour in batter. Bake at 350 degrees for about 50 minutes.

(Contributed by Charlene Mathews and her family)

Gagnon's Banana Bread

6-7 of G'Dad's finger bananas or some from the store
3/4 cup white sugar
1 teaspoon salt
1/2 cup chopped nuts
3 eggs
2 cups flour
1 teaspoon baking soda

Peel and mash bananas. Mix all ingredients together in bowl, then spoon into greased loaf pan. Bake at 350 degrees for 1 hour. Invert (turn the loaf pan upside down) on a wire rack to cool. Freezes well.

My Daddy

I had a wonderful daddy,
The greatest to ever walk the earth.
He thought that I was perfect,
From the first moment of my birth.

We shared almost everything.
He guided me, encouraged me,
And protected me in every possible way.
He carried me when I was tired,
Kissed away my hurts and dried my tears.

As I grew older he encouraged me in every way,
And his trust was complete.
I nearly broke his heart when I grew up and married,
Until he finally realized that I would always be his
"little girl".

I wish that every child could have a daddy like mine,
But I am sure that God made only a few as precious as
"My Daddy".

Jeannine Browning

Fun Things To Do

Ginny and Tricia

Fun Things To Do

Colleen's Old Family Recipe for Play Dough

1 cup water
1 cup flour
1/2 cup salt
2 teaspoons cream of tartar
1 Tablespoon vegetable oil
Food coloring

Put water, flour, salt, cream of tartar and vegetable oil in a pot and place on the stove burner.

Cook over medium heat. Stir until the mixture thickens. Add food coloring.

Pour out on kitchen counter and knead until smooth. Will keep several months in a tightly sealed container.

(Knead means to push, mash and pull on the play dough until it is smooth.)

(This recipe is from my wonderful sister, Colleen Barton, who lives in Tallahasse, Florida.)

Homemade Raisins

1 bunch seedless grapes

Wash grapes and pull off stems. Place on a cookie sheet. Place cookie sheet in the sun until they have shrunk and dried to be "Homemade Raisins".

Sue Fetner, owner of Country Beginnings gave me this idea. I asked where she put the cookie sheet so that no bugs, etc. got on the grapes. Her wonderful answer was, "I ride them around in the back window of my car until they are raisins!" You just can't beat that! I love it!

The source of an untroubled heart is God.

Chocolate Pretzels

12 ounces semi-sweet chocolate
1/2 ounce paraffin, grated
60 unbroken thin salty pretzels

In a heavy saucepan, slowly melt chocolate and paraffin over low heat. Let mixture stand for 5 minutes before dipping pretzels in. Dip each pretzel in chocolate, coating well; remove carefully with a fork or tongs. Allow to cool on a sheet of waxed paper. If chocolate becomes too thick, return to heat until it softens again.

(Note — You can dip half of the pretzel in chocolate and leave the other half plain.)

Peggy's Letter Pretzels

1 Tablespoon yeast
1/2 cup warm water
1 teaspoon honey
1 teaspoon salt
1 1/3 cups all purpose flour
Coarse salt, if possible
1 egg

Dissolve yeast in 1/2 cup warm water. Add honey and salt and mix well. Then add flour and knead. Roll pieces to form letters. Place on baking sheet and brush with beaten egg. Sprinkle with coarse salt.

Bake for 10 minutes in preheated 425 degree oven.

Bubble Gum Ice Cream

Homemade Ice Cream (recipe on page 125)
Chicklets bubble gum

Make vanilla ice cream in churn. When finished (ice cream is firm) remove paddle and add in several packets of chicklets, stir well.

Happy Bath Time

10-20 drops of food coloring of your choice

Stop up the drain in the bath tub, begin adding your bath water and add the food coloring at the same time. This makes a beautiful tub of fun water to play in (hopefully getting clean at the same time).

(No, it does not color your child. I have done this with four children and five grandchildren and I haven't gotten a green or blue one yet!)

For the Birds

Buy or make a bird feeder for your back yard. The whole family will enjoy watching the different kinds of birds eating at your feeder.

The Blue Jays are always searching for shelled peanuts or sunflower seeds. They make a big show of pushing around the seeds they don't want...most of those fall on the ground where the quail and dove are happy to eat them.

Woodpeckers of all sorts will also eat from your feeder, but they have different feet and can't sit on the perch. They look like they are hanging on for dear life, but their feet are made for clutching the side of a tree, and they are comfortable hanging on the perch while they eat.

Keep a special pad and pencil handy so you can keep a record of each new kind of bird who uses your feeder, and how many different kinds drop by.

I keep my feeder on a stand about 5 feet from my kitchen window where I can watch without scaring some of the shy birds. The bird feeder is mine (a special stand made by Paul and Leah Casper for me), but slowly my husband, children and grandchildren got hooked on watching the different birds and now it is a family love.

Peanut Butter Pine Cones

Large, open pine cone
1/2 cup peanut butter
1/2 cup cornmeal
1 cup small birdseed
Heavy twine (string)

Combine cornmeal, peanut butter and seeds; mix well. Tie a 5-foot to 8-foot length of twine to the top of the opened pine cone. Fill every opening in the pine cone with the peanut butter mixture. Tie end of twine to a tree branch. Sit back and watch the birds enjoy their special treat.

Shaving Cream Fun

Cover the top of a formica table (or any table that moisture won't hurt) with shaving cream. This is a form of finger painting. Just take a finger or two and begin your art work. When you are finished, just smooth out the shaving cream again and start all over. Be creative!

When you are finished just wipe off the table removing all the shaving cream. No harm is done to the table, and it is clean!

(Contributed by Sue Fetner)

Fun Places To Go

To a movie
Swimming...in a pool, lake or ocean
Skiing...on water, or snow
Hiking
To a local pond to feed the ducks or fish (use stale bread or dry oatmeal)
Go to a local nursing home to visit someone who does not have a family (take them a flower)
Skating...roller or ice (with family or friends)
Have a picnic in a park (or in your backyard). (Just spread an old blanket under a tree, eat your lunch and enjoy the beauty around you.)
If you are planning a picnic in the park and it begins to rain, have your picnic inside. You can still have a great time.
Go for a bike ride with family or friends. Take along a snack that travels well.
Visit someone in your neighborhood that seems lonely. (Ask your mother first!) Take them a flower from your yard or some fresh cookies you have just baked!

Be creative! Don't sit around and moan because you are bored and don't have anything to do! There is always something wonderful and exciting to do if you just follow some of the above ideas, or think up some of your own! Have fun! Be happy!

The Great Surprise!

What fun to have a scavenger hunt for Dad and Mom's Christmas gifts from you. The first clue is in a note, tied with a pretty ribbon, hanging from the Christmas Tree.

(For example)
"I knew you'd read me
sooner or later.
Now look by the eggs
in the refrigerator."

Clue #2 is in the refrigerator stuck on to the egg container.

"Now please don't stop
You're in for some fun.
Look out by the tree
That's right in the sun."

Under a tree in the back yard is a special gift you have for someone you love.

(You could also hide your dad's gift in the garage or his workshop. Choose any place to hide a gift for your mom, dad, sister, brother, grandparents that is special for you or for them. Have fun!)

(Make up your own poems if you can, or get another family member to help you. Use your imagination!)

(Contributed by Lindy Hazel Taylor)

Love Me, Love My Dog!

How to take good care of you dog when he/she has a stomach ache, or a growling stomach. (When your dog is vomiting or seems nauseated.)

Give your dog a bowl of cottage cheese. Your dog will love it and unless there is a serious problem, that will be that! I have been using this method for over 20 years and it has never failed me or my pooch! If your dog continues to have a problem take him/her to see your veterinarian.

Gator

Little Scotty's Favorite Recipe

1 cup of flour
1 pound of patience
Make sure that you stir well.
2 candy canes
1 gentle hug
Till sweetness you can smell.
A dash of sugar
A load of love
It'll be real good, you'll see.
Bake till it's done
And then you have
Precious memories for Mommy and Me!

Julie Casper Clifton

Paper Bag Masks

Take a paper bag large enough to fit over your head. Cut holes in the bag for your eyes, nose and mouth.

You can decorate the bag with crayons or magic markers.

Add feathers, ribbons, glued on buttons or anything else you have to make your mask complete.

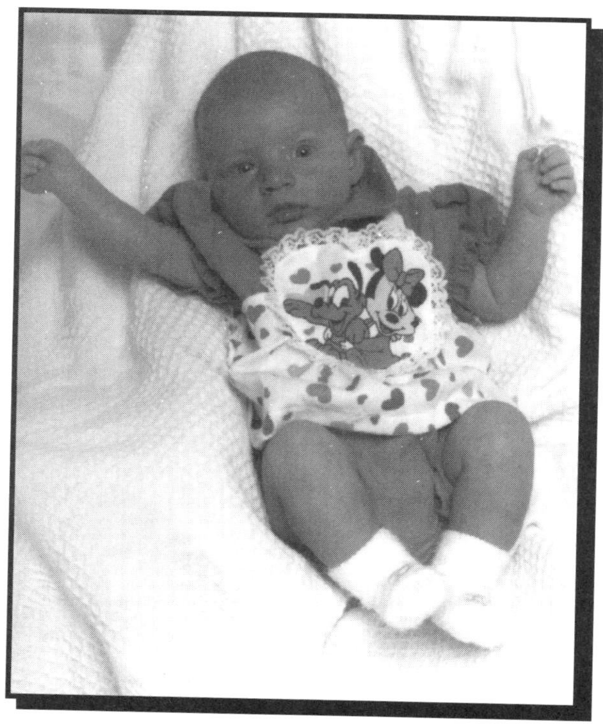

Shelby Browning

Take time to enjoy each day!

Games

The Gang

Games

Clothes Pins in a Bottle

1 quart glass milk bottle (or any 1 quart jar)
6 clothes pins for each player

Stand about 1 or 2 feet away from the milk bottle. Stand up straight! See how many clothes pins you can drop into the milk bottle. The player with the most pins in the bottle wins.

You may have to adjust your rules just a little if players are of different sizes and ages. Try to make it fair for everyone.

He who ruleth well his heart,
And keeps his temper down,
Will be a better, wiser part,
Than he who takes the town.

Relay Races

Choose two teams with an even number of players on each side.

Egg on Spoon Relay Race

2 raw eggs
2 Tablespoons
(Extra raw eggs in case the first two are broken)

Hold one end of the spoon in your mouth and put the egg in the other. Try to get it to the next person on your team without dropping or breaking the egg. No running. Walking is important! (Smaller children can also do this race by holding the spoon in their hands.)

Grapefruit under Chin

2 large grapefruits (or oranges)

Divided into teams. Walk to the next team player. They have to remove the grapefruit from under your chin by taking it between their chin and chest. If dropped you are out.

Candy Count (Game)

Fill a small jar (baby food jar size) with candy corn. Empty jar and count each piece of candy. Return candy to jar when counted. Write down the total in a safe place. Tie a ribbon around lid of jar.

Do the same with a medium jar filled with different candy. Repeat with a larger jar. Place the 3 jars on a table where everyone can see them. Put a clean sheet of paper in front of each jar. Put as many numbers down the left side of the page as there are children at the party. Let each child make a guess as to the total number of pieces of candy in each jar...even if you have to write it down for them. The person who comes closest without going over wins the jar of candy.

This can also be done with adults. It isn't as easy as you might think...but the children love it!

Funny Answers

Each player gets a piece of paper and a pencil. They must write their name at the top and number from 1 thru 10 on the left side of the paper.

The leader will ask everyone to write their answer next to the correct number.

1. Give a number from 17 to 70.
2. Give the name of a favorite movie actress or actor (girls-actress, boys-actor).
3. Give a number from 17 to 50.
4. Write down a color.
5. Write down the name of any profession (the kind of work someone does).
6. Give the name of a city any place in the world.
7. Name any place in your town.
8. Give a number from 1 to 20.
9. Give a number from 18 to 30.
10. Name a vegetable.

After all these instructions are read and filled in, the players exchange papers. The leader reads out loud the following list of questions, one at a time. After the question is read, each player takes a turn reading out loud the answer on the paper they have, and tell who wrote that paper.

1. At what age will you get married?
2. Who will she (or he) look like?
3. How old will your wife (or husband) be?
4. What color eyes will she (or he) have?
5. What business will you be in then?
6. In what city will you live?
7. Where will you meet your husband or wife?
8. How many children will you have?
9. At what age will you graduate from college?
10. What will you serve at your wedding?

How Good is your Memory

10-15 articles that are found in your home, or school
Pencils and paper for everyone
Tray to put articles on and something to cover everything

Place 10-15 articles on a tray and cover so that nothing can be seen.

Give each player a pencil and paper. When you are ready, give the signal and uncover the tray. Leave everything exposed for three minutes while everyone playing gets a good look, and tries to remember what they have seen. No one may write anything during this time.

When the three minutes are up, cover the tray again so that nothing can be seen. The players now have five minutes to write down on their papers the names of what they have seen on the tray. Stop everyone from writing when time is up!

The person who has the most correct answers wins the prize. (In case someone finishes early and feels sure they have all the correct answers they can yell "finished!"

Red Rover, Red Rover

1. Choose sides and captains.
2. Line up with teams facing each other.
3. Team members hold hands or wrists to form a line.
4. Team one calls one person from other team to try to break through their line. Call — Red Rover, Red Rover, Let ____ come over!
5. Person whose name was called comes running over and tries to break through line.
6. If runner breaks through he/she chooses one person to return with him/her to Team Two. If runner does not break through he joins Team One.
7. Keep going until all members, except one, are on one team.

This can be a rough game, so be sure that players are the same size.

"Secret Story" Game

Paper and pencils

Take turns writing a secret story, usually using the names of each person in the car (or in your family) leaving blanks for adjectives to be filled in. When the story is completed, each person will take a turn saying any adjective and the story writer will fill in the blanks with each persons contribution. This involves much laughing and happiness and tends to make a long trip seem shorter.

(In later years one could buy "Mad Libs" printed on a tablet that was based on the same idea, but not nearly as much fun as our game!)

(Contributed by Gee Gee Wood and her family)

Through the Hoop

An embroidery hoop (any size, or anything round like an embroidery hoop)
A small ball
A small piece of string or twine

Tie a piece of string to the embroidery hoop, then tape or tie the other end of the string or twine in the middle of an open doorway. Let the hoop hang down until about eye level for you.

Mark an area about 6 feet away from the doorway. Stand behind the mark and see how many times out of six throws that you can get the ball through the hoop. If you have more than one player you will need to take turns, the first one getting 10 balls through the hoop wins.

Note — Very small children will need to throw from 4 or 5 feet away.

Egg-Carton Pitch

Need something different to do? Well here is a fun game that only takes a few buttons or other tiny objects and an egg carton.

Take an empty egg-carton and cut off the cover. Take a crayon or magic marker and number the sections of the egg-carton from 1 thru 12. You can number them in any order you choose.

You can play by yourself, or in teams. Place the egg-carton on a straight chair. Stand about 6 feet away from the chair and see how many buttons you can get in the sections of the egg carton. Each player has three buttons to play with. Each player scores the number of points into which the button falls. The person or team with the most points wins.

Easter

See how many words you can make out of Easter in 5 or 10 minutes. You can play this by yourself, or several can play. The first one with the most words in a given time is the winner.

Examples:
Set
Sat
Eat
Star
Rat
Steer
Rest
Ate
Are
Tease

You can only use the exact letters found in the word.

It is fun to see how many words you can make out of Thanksgiving, Christmas, Valentine's Day, or your own name. Be creative!

Sue's Gingerbread Man Hunt

The children at Sue Fetner's Country Beginnings always have a lot of fun, and one such "fun" idea is to have a Gingerbread Man Hunt.

The children and teachers make a large Gingerbread Man and place him in the oven to bake. While he is baking and everyone is doing something else, the Gingerbread Man escapes from the oven. When everyone returns to the oven to remove the Gingerbread Man they discover that he has escaped. All that is there is a note telling them he has run away. The note could say:

"I have run away and you can't find me,
Look for me in the ______tree." (Name your own favorite tree or the kind in your yard.)
When you look in the _______ tree you will find another note from the Gingerbread Man. (Write another hint as to where he might be found.)

When you get to the final place you will finally find the Gingerbread Man, and he can be eaten!

Write as many clues as you can think up...the more, the better.

My Mother

My Mother is the one
Who cared for me each day,
She is the precious one
Who taught me to kneel and pray.

A mother's love knows no end,
She taught me right from wrong.
She taught me to set my goals and never bend,
She taught me to sing a joyful song.

She cared for me when I was sick,
She loved me whether I was good or bad.
She is the most wonderful mother,
Any child has ever had.

Jeannine Browning, 1993

Family Fun

Birthday Candle Fun
Kevin blowing out birthday candles while everyone else waits their turn.

Family Fun

Birthday Candles

We always let the birthday child blow out all the candles first, then each child present at the birthday party got their turn. This may take a while to do this at a large party, but the kids love it, and have as much fun doing this as playing a game. After all, we are building memories, aren't we?

Making Butter

1/2 pint whipping cream
1 empty pint jar
Pinch of salt

Pour whipping cream into jar and cover tightly. Shake vigorously (real hard) until butter forms. Pour off any liquid. Add salt and stir a little. Serve on crackers or fresh bread. Yum!

Hallowe'en Party (Home or School)

Shopping List:

2 gallons fresh orange juice (if possible)
Chocolate Cake Mix (24 cupcakes)
24 cupcake liners
3 flavors frosting mix
3-6 different toppings (Sprinkles, chocolate chips, coconut, candy, etc.)
Punch bowl and ladle
24 plastic cups
24 napkins
24 plastic or paper plates
24 plastic forks
24 plastic spoons (for decorating cupcakes)
Containers for each child to have their own frosting mix, etc. to decorate cupcakes
Wet wipes for each child

Bake cupcakes day before party. Let children at party decorate cupcakes. Make an ice ring with orange juice and plastic spiders.

Easter Bird Nest with Jelly Bean Eggs

3 cups krispy rice cereal
1 cup coconut

Combine first two ingredients in a medium bowl.

1/3 cup light corn syrup
1/2 cup brown sugar
3/4 cup smooth peanut butter
1 teaspoon vanilla

Combine next four ingredients in a medium pot and bring to a boil while stirring.

Remove from heat and stir in cereal and coconut. Let cool until just slightly warm. Shape into balls, then into small bird nests by poking finger into ball and spreading hole bigger to make a nest. Fill hole with 3-5 small jelly bean "eggs".

(Contributed by Tricia and Justin Mast)

Popsicles

1 package Kool-aid (sweetened)

Make Kool-aid according to package directions. Pour into small plastic containers or cups. Insert small plastic spoons or plastic or wooden ice cream sticks and freeze. Small kids love these on warm days.

(Contributed by Dick and Dee Burner)

Peanut Butter

1 pound raw peanuts
2 Tablespoons vegetable oil (more if needed)
1/4 teaspoon salt

Roast raw peanuts at 300 degrees for 40 minutes. Shell and take hulls off each peanut. Put 1 cup peanuts in blender. Add 2 tablespoons vegetable oil and 1/4 teaspoon salt. Grind and mix until smooth. Eat on crackers or apple slices.

Scented Cinnamon Ornaments

4 ounce can cinnamon (approximately 1 cup)
1 Tablespoon ground cloves
1 Tablespoon nutmeg
3/4 cup applesauce (smooth)
2 Tablespoons white glue

In medium bowl combine spices. Add applesauce and glue; stir to combine. Work mixture with hands for 2-3 minutes or until smooth and ingredients are completely mixed. Divide into four balls. Roll out each ball of dough until it is about 1/4 inch in thickness. Cut dough with a metal cookie cutter. Use a straw or a toothpick to make a hole in the top of each ornament, if you want to hang your ornament.

Place cutouts on a closely woven wire rack and dry at room temperature for several days. Turn ornaments over once each day until completely dry. Decorate with thin ribbons, tiny flowers, etc. DO NOT EAT! (I made these over two years ago and they are still as beautiful as ever, and even still smell good!)

Pumpkin Time

Pick out your own pumpkin from a field, if possible, for Halloween and Thanksgiving. Make a special trip to a pumpkin field if there is one in your area, if not go to a pumpkin stand. Let your child or children choose the pumpkin to carve a Jack-O-Lantern. Buy two large pumpkins while you are there and save one for Thanksgiving and making fresh pumpkin pie.

Thanksgiving in Webster

We always celebrated Thanksgiving at our grandparents home until they were too old to carry on the elaborate traditions.

We always had a huge, wonderfully baked fresh turkey, hot and mild corn bread dressing, delicious gravy, conch peas with hot pepper sauce, fresh fruit salad, roasted pecans, cranberry sauce, celery stuffed with cream cheese and pecan slivers, slavery bread, fresh coconut cake, plain pound cake, pecan and pumpkin pies and ambrosia.

Everyone always waddled away from the table in absolute misery from eating too much. Everyone except Papa (my grandfather). He was always the one with the self-control. He was able to leave one bite of food on his plate if he was full, or happily refuse dessert. Not the rest of us, we gorged and were miserable. I always admired my grandfathers self-control, but never could understand how he could turn down a yummy dessert.

Christmas in Florida

Try to find a place where your family can go together to cut down your Christmas tree. If this is not possible take the whole family along to a tree lot to help choose your special tree.

When we were kids in Webster, Florida we always went out to our ranch with our grandfather during the summer and chose our tree for Christmas time. It always had to be the most beautiful tree we could find.

Several days before Christmas, Papa (our wonderful grandfather) loaded us up in the back of his truck and off we went to cut down our special tree. Usually it was there waiting for us, but on more than one occasion someone had sneaked out on the ranch and stolen our tree. We were heartbroken at first, but somehow Papa always managed to lead us to another almost perfect tree. He cut the tree down and we all helped him load it on his truck. We laughed and sang at the top of our voices all the way home where our mother and grandmother waited for the special tree.

(A wonderful, happy memory.)

Child's Birthday Party Invitation

Have a member of your family or someone you know draw an invitation according to the theme of your child's birthday party. On the inside write the necessary information and ask the guest to color the invitation and bring to the birthday party. The one who does the best job of coloring the invitation gets a special prize.

Index

Jeannine B. Browning
Cookbooks by Jeannine
8552 Sylvan Drive
Melbourne, Florida 32904-2426

Please send ____ copies of ***Kids At Work*** .... @ $12.95 each ________
Please send ____ copies of ***Sand In My Shoes*** .... @ 14.95 each ________
Please send ____ copies of ***Florida Fixin's*** .... @ 9.95 each ________
Florida residents add 6% sales tax .... ________
Add UPS and handling .... @ 2.50 each ________
Total $ ____________

☐ Check or money order enclosed.
Please charge to ☐ Mastercard ☐ Visa ☐ Discover
Card Number ____
Expiration date __________ Signature ____________________________

From:
Name ____________________
Address ____________________
City ____________________
State __________ Zip __________
Phone Number ( ) __________
(No P.O. Boxes)

Ship to:
Name ____________________
Address ____________________
City ____________________
State __________ Zip __________

Jeannine B. Browning
Cookbooks by Jeannine
8552 Sylvan Drive
Melbourne, Florida 32904-2426

Please send ____ copies of ***Kids At Work*** .... @ $12.95 each ________
Please send ____ copies of ***Sand In My Shoes*** .... @ 14.95 each ________
Please send ____ copies of ***Florida Fixin's*** .... @ 9.95 each ________
Florida residents add 6% sales tax .... ________
Add UPS and handling .... @ 2.50 each ________
Total $ ____________

☐ Check or money order enclosed.
Please charge to ☐ Mastercard ☐ Visa ☐ Discover
Card Number ____
Expiration date __________ Signature ____________________________

From:
Name ____________________
Address ____________________
City ____________________
State __________ Zip __________
Phone Number ( ) __________
(No P.O. Boxes)

Ship to:
Name ____________________
Address ____________________
City ____________________
State __________ Zip __________